EMPOWERMENT OF
BUSINESS IDENTITY

Empowerment for phlebotomy program

By: Monica Young

Write your name: _____

As your reading you will be applying this book to your lifestyle and please let me know if we can help with your career.

DEDICATION

To my mother, Rebecca Sapp, and my father, Theodore Sapp—my two heroes.

Without my parents, I wouldn't be the woman I am today. I thank God for both of them. Even though I didn't always understand the way they raised me or the choices they made, I know deep down that everything they did helped shape me for the better. Through moments of confusion, one truth remained clear: God placed them in my life to help me grow into the person I was meant to be.

My mother and father are two of the hardest-working people I've ever known. They never quit, never backed down, and always gave their best to whatever they set out to do. That spirit of perseverance, I believe, lives in me too. My ambition, my growth, and my resilience are reflections of their strength—and for that, I am forever grateful.

This book is especially dedicated to my beautiful mother, who is no longer with us. Mommy, I know if you were here, you would be proud of me. I can feel your love even now, and I hope you feel mine too. Thank you for the love, care, and nourishment you poured into me, even when things weren't perfect. I know you always loved me—and I love you just as deeply.

And to my father—Daddy, you're my rock. My buddy. Every little girl loves her daddy, no matter what anyone says. That bond we share means the world to me.

I love you both dearly. You are phenomenal parents, and this book is a manifestation to the foundation you provided for me.

The Bible verse about honoring your father and mother is Exodus 20:12, which states,

"Honor your father and your mother, that your days may be long in the land that the Lord your God is giving your."

Ephesians 6:2-3 also states that this is God's first commandment with a promise about honoring your mother and father.

PROLOGUE

In today's healthcare environment, the role of the phlebotomist is evolving rapidly. No longer confined to hospital labs or clinics, phlebotomists are stepping into entrepreneurial roles, creating mobile businesses that deliver critical services right where patients need them. This shift is both exciting and daunting. It calls for more than clinical skill—it demands leadership, resilience, business acumen, and a mindset geared toward growth.

Coaching a Successful Phlebotomist: The Empowerment Program is designed to meet that demand. This book isn't just a manual; it's an invitation to a transformational journey where you reclaim your professional power and expand your impact. At its heart, the program underscores that success in mobile phlebotomy is not just about drawing blood—it's about drawing out your fullest potential as a confident, accountable, and faith-driven entrepreneur.

The essence of this work lies in empowerment—the process of gaining control over your professional destiny by developing new skills, fostering accountability, and embracing a mindset of continuous improvement. It recognizes that running a mobile phlebotomy business requires more than technical proficiency; it calls for courage to step into uncertainty, flexibility to adapt, and a strong foundation of faith and integrity to sustain you.

Coaching emerges here as a key catalyst. It provides a structured, supportive relationship that challenges complacency and nurtures progress. It's about guiding you through the complexities of business ownership with clarity and compassion. Accountability, then, becomes your daily practice—an honest commitment to showing up fully for your goals and for those who rely on your services.

This book also invites you to view challenges not as obstacles but as opportunities to grow stronger. In the unpredictable world of entrepreneurship, resilience isn't optional; it's essential. You'll learn how to navigate setbacks with grace, adjust your course with insight, and keep your vision alive through determination.

Above all, this program emphasizes the profound role of faith in your journey. Trusting in God's guidance doesn't just provide comfort—it fuels perseverance and inspires meaningful action. It reminds you that while you put in the work, you're never truly alone on this path.

As you begin this program, I encourage you to embrace each chapter not as an endpoint but as a stepping stone. Allow yourself to be challenged and supported. Draw on the tools and wisdom offered here to build a mobile phlebotomy business that not only succeeds financially but also honors your purpose and values.

Your journey to empowerment starts now.

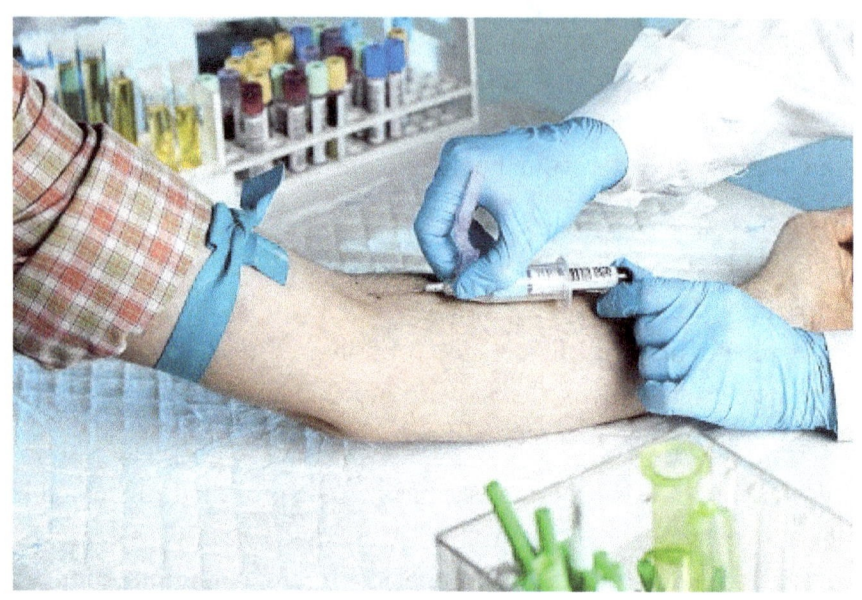

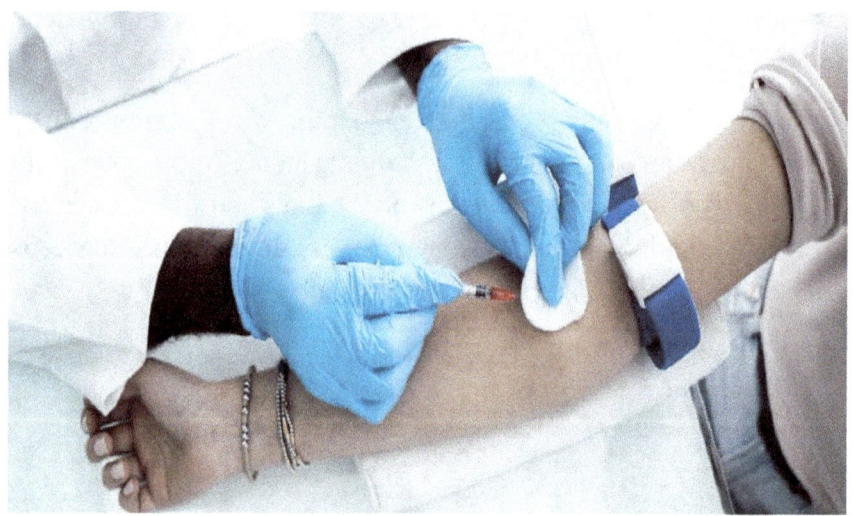

TABLE OF CONTENTS

INTRODUCTION

Becoming a phlebotomist is more than just learning to draw blood. It's about touching lives, building trust, and being a calming presence during what can be an anxious moment for many patients. But what if your skills could take you even further? What if, beyond mastering the craft of phlebotomy, you could also become your own boss, grow a thriving business, and build a life of purpose—grounded in faith and driven by determination?

"I can do all this through Him who gives me strength."

— Philippians 4:13

That's what this book is all about.

Coaching a Successful Phlebotomist: The Empowerment Program is not your typical guide to venipuncture and certification. This is a roadmap for those who want to do more than just work a job—it's for those who feel called to lead, to serve, and to create something lasting. Whether you're just beginning your phlebotomy journey or you've been in the field for years and are ready to take your next big step, this book was written for you.

You'll find no complicated jargon here. Instead, what you'll discover are practical steps, thoughtful guidance, and stories grounded in real experience. You'll learn how coaching can help you unlock your potential, how accountability fuels real growth, and how building your business starts with building yourself. Most importantly, you'll see how faith—yes, real, honest, leaning-on-God kind of faith—can carry you through every challenge.

This book walks you through five essential areas:

- **In Chapter 1**, you'll learn how coaching works—not just as a support system, but as a powerful, structured partnership that helps you stay focused and move forward. You'll see how even simple tools like pre-call forms and monthly reviews can change the way you grow, both as a phlebotomist and as a leader.

- **In Chapter 2**, we'll talk about accountability—not as punishment, but as power. You'll see why holding yourself accountable is the difference between dreaming and doing, and how small, consistent actions can bring about big results in your business.

- **In Chapter 3**, we'll dive into the nuts and bolts of starting your mobile phlebotomy business. From getting your paperwork in order to crafting a solid business plan and standing out in a growing market, you'll get a step-by-step look at what it takes to lay a strong foundation.

- **In Chapter 4**, we'll talk about what it really means to feel empowered. It's not just about confidence—it's about having the courage to keep going when things get hard, the clarity to set meaningful goals, and the willingness to take full responsibility for your success.

- And finally, **Chapter 5** brings us back to the heart of it all— **faith**. Because no matter how strong your skills are or how detailed your business plan is, there will be moments of uncertainty. Trusting God's guidance doesn't mean sitting back—it means moving forward with peace, even when you can't see the full picture.

Throughout this journey, you'll be reminded that success doesn't happen overnight. It's built day by day, with effort, patience, and heart. The Empowerment Program is here to walk with you, step by step, as you grow into the confident, skilled, faith-rooted business owner you were meant to be.

So, whether you're reading this with a stethoscope around your neck or a notebook full of business ideas, take a deep breath. You are not alone in this. You have the tools. You have the passion. And now, you have the guidance.

Let's begin.

CHAPTER ONE
How Coaching Works

Embarking on the journey to become a successful phlebotomist and business owner is both exciting and challenging. It's not just about mastering the technical skills of blood collection; it's about cultivating an entrepreneurial mindset, embracing accountability, and staying committed to your goals. This is where coaching becomes invaluable.

Understanding Coaching in Phlebotomy

Coaching is a collaborative process where a coach supports you in achieving your personal and professional goals. In the context of phlebotomy, coaching goes beyond teaching you how to draw blood; it helps you develop the mindset and skills needed to run a successful mobile phlebotomy business.

The Empowerment Coaching Program is designed to guide you through this journey by focusing on three key areas:

- **Preparation**: Laying a strong foundation for your business.

- **Responsibility**: Taking ownership of your actions and decisions.

- **Follow-through**: Ensuring consistent progress toward your goals.

The GROW Model: A Structured Approach to Coaching

One effective framework used in coaching is the GROW model:

- **Goal**: Define what you want to achieve.

- **Reality**: Assess your current situation.

- **Options**: Explore possible strategies to reach your goal.

- **Way Forward**: Decide on the actions to take.

This model provides a clear structure for coaching sessions, ensuring that each conversation is purposeful and directed toward achieving specific outcomes.

The Importance of Preparation

Effective coaching begins with preparation. Before each session, both you and your coach should complete a pre-call form. This form helps identify the topics to be discussed, any challenges faced, and the goals for the upcoming session. Research indicates that preparatory work enhances the effectiveness of coaching relationships, as it ensures both parties are aligned and focused.

For instance, if you're struggling with time management, the pre-call form might highlight this issue, allowing your coach to tailor the session to address it specifically. This targeted approach maximizes the value of each coaching interaction.

Accountability: The Cornerstone of Success

Accountability is crucial in coaching. It involves setting clear expectations and holding yourself responsible for meeting them. In the Empowerment Coaching Program, accountability is integrated into the coaching process through:

- **Setting SMART Goals**: Goals should be Specific, Measurable, Achievable, Relevant, and Time-bound. This clarity makes it easier to track progress and stay motivated.

- **Creating Action Plans**: Breaking down goals into smaller, manageable tasks with defined timelines helps prevent overwhelm and ensures consistent progress.

- **Regular Check-Ins**: Scheduled sessions provide opportunities to review progress, discuss challenges, and adjust plans as needed. These check-ins reinforce commitment and keep you on track.

For example, if your goal is to complete the necessary paperwork to start your mobile phlebotomy business, your coach might help break this down into tasks such as researching licensing requirements, filling out forms, and submitting applications. Regular check-ins ensure these tasks are completed on time and any obstacles are addressed promptly.

Commitment: Taking Ownership

Becoming a successful phlebotomist is not just about completing a training course or passing an exam. It's about showing up consistently—with professionalism, care, and a drive to improve every day. In the Empowerment Coaching Program, *commitment* means taking full responsibility for your growth not only as a healthcare provider but as a future business owner.

For aspiring mobile phlebotomists, this may look like committing to:

- Practicing your venipuncture technique until it becomes second nature.

- Showing up early to appointments with all the necessary supplies.

- Following up with clients and partners to build strong, reliable relationships.

- Staying up to date on healthcare regulations and maintaining your certifications.

- Putting in the effort to create a strong business foundation, even when you're tired or discouraged.

Coaching helps turn that commitment into action. With support and guidance, you're held accountable to your goals—whether that's launching your own mobile service, expanding your client list, or improving your service quality. The most successful phlebotomists aren't just skilled—they're dependable, motivated, and prepared. That kind of commitment begins with mindset and follows through with action.

Monthly Reviews: A Mirror for Your Growth

In the life of a busy phlebotomist, it's easy to stay stuck in "go mode"—rushing from one appointment to the next, juggling paperwork, phone calls, and maybe even family responsibilities. That's why the monthly review in the Empowerment Coaching Program isn't just another item on your to-do list—it's your chance to pause, breathe, and reflect.

Think of it as holding up a mirror to your progress. What's working? What's not? Where are you growing—and where are you getting stuck?

These monthly sessions are designed to do three powerful things:

1. **Celebrate your wins**—big or small. Whether it's finally getting your first repeat client, mastering a tricky venipuncture, or just staying organized for four weeks straight, these moments matter.

2. **Spot trouble early**—like a dip in motivation, a gap in your schedule, or a process that's not quite working (such as delayed follow-ups or too much time lost on admin tasks).

3. **Refocus your energy**—by adjusting goals, refreshing strategies, and creating new action steps that reflect your growth.

"May the favor of the Lord our God rest on us; establish the work of our hands for us—yes, establish the work of our hands."

— Psalm 90:17

This scripture beautifully captures the heart of these reviews. You're not just evaluating progress—you're inviting God to bless, affirm, and build upon the work you've done. Each reflection is a chance to partner with Him in refining your mission and advancing your purpose.

Let's say you've built a decent client list, but you're constantly overbooked or scrambling with last-minute changes. A monthly review could help you see patterns in your scheduling, explore whether it's time to invest in software, or even talk through outsourcing help. The goal is to make your business serve *you*, not drain you.

But perhaps more importantly, these reviews remind you why you started. In the rush of tasks, it's easy to forget that you're not just collecting samples—you're building something. A life. A legacy. A business rooted in service, skill, and faith.

With each review, you become more than a technician—you grow into the confident, capable leader of your own mobile phlebotomy practice.

Overcoming Roadblocks

Starting and growing a phlebotomy business isn't always smooth. You'll hit bumps in the road—missed appointments, difficult clients, unexpected delays in getting licenses, or even moments of self-doubt. These are all part of the process.

That's why one of the core purposes of coaching is helping you face challenges head-on, not avoid them.

In your coaching sessions, you'll learn how to:

- Identify what's really holding you back. Is it time management? Fear of failure? A lack of clarity on next steps?
- Break big challenges into smaller, more manageable tasks.
- Create solutions that fit your lifestyle and values.

For example, if you're struggling to find clients, a coach can help you build a realistic outreach plan—whether that means improving your social media, refining your pitch to clinics, or offering a special promotion to get your name out there.

And when a technical mistake happens—like mishandling a sample or being late to an appointment—coaching helps you learn from it, not get stuck in shame or frustration. Mistakes don't define you. How you respond to them does.

Roadblocks are not the end of the road. With the right coaching, they become learning opportunities that build your confidence, resilience, and professional identity.

The Role of Faith in Coaching

In the Empowerment Program, we believe that building a successful phlebotomy career is not just a business goal—it's a calling. And like any calling, it requires faith.

Faith isn't just about spirituality. It's about believing that your work has meaning. It's about trusting that the effort you're putting in—those early mornings, long days, and hard conversations—will bear fruit. It's knowing that you are not doing this alone.

As Proverbs 3:5-6 reminds us:

"Trust in the Lord with all your heart and lean not on your own understanding; in all your ways acknowledge Him, and He shall direct your paths."

When starting a phlebotomy business, faith becomes your anchor:

- When clients cancel appointments, you stay steady.

- When income is slow, you keep showing up and planting seeds.

- When self-doubt creeps in, you remember why you started this journey.

Faith also influences how you treat others. A successful phlebotomist with strong faith brings compassion, patience, and integrity to every interaction—with clients, partners, and employees. This becomes your reputation—and in healthcare, your reputation is everything.

By keeping God at the center of your journey, you're not only building a business—you're building a life of purpose.

Conclusion: Empowered to Succeed

Coaching is a powerful tool for personal and professional development. In the context of phlebotomy, it provides the guidance and support needed to transition from a skilled technician to a successful business owner. By embracing preparation, accountability, commitment, and faith, you can navigate the challenges of entrepreneurship and achieve your goals.

The Empowerment Coaching Program offers a structured, supportive framework to help you unlock your potential and build a thriving mobile phlebotomy business. With the right guidance and mindset, success is within reach.

References

- Wikipedia contributors. (2025). *Coaching*. Wikipedia. Retrieved from https://en.wikipedia.org/wiki/Coaching

- Wikipedia contributors. (2025). *GROW model*. Wikipedia. Retrieved from https://en.wikipedia.org/wiki/GROW_model

- The Knowledge Academy. (2025). *What is Coaching? A Comprehensive Guide*. Retrieved from https://www.theknowledgeacademy.com/blog/what-is-coaching/

- HR Fraternity. (2025). *Empowering Clients to Set Achievable Goals in Coaching Sessions*. Retrieved from https://www.hrfraternity.com/health-excellence/empowering-clients-to-set-achievable-goals-in-coaching-sessions.html

- Learn Business. (2025). *How to Foster Accountability in Coaching Sessions*. Retrieved from https://learn-business.org/coaching/foster-accountability-coaching-sessions/

- Robin Waite. (2025). *Cultivating Progress: Strategies for Effectively Coaching Clients*. Retrieved from https://www.robinwaite.com/blog/cultivating-progress-strategies-for-effectively-coaching-clients

- EMOCARE. (2025). *Accountability Coaching: Achieving Goals with Support and Guidance*. Retrieved from https://emocare.co.in/accountability-coaching

CHAPTER TWO
HOLDING YOURSELF ACCOUNTABLE

Accountability is more than just a buzzword—it's the bedrock of sustainable success. As an aspiring mobile phlebotomist and entrepreneur, you're not just learning how to draw blood; you're learning how to manage your time, follow through on commitments, and keep your word—to yourself, your clients, and your business. In the Empowerment Coaching Program, accountability is not about pressure or punishment. It's about creating a system where your actions align with your goals and your vision becomes reality.

Accountability in Entrepreneurship: Being Your Own Boss (for Real)

When you launch your own mobile phlebotomy business, you quickly realize that being your own boss isn't just about setting your own hours or choosing your clients. It also means there's no supervisor making sure your lab kits are stocked, your vehicle is clean and ready, or that your samples are dropped off on time. There's no one double-checking if you followed up on that physician referral or renewed your CLIA waiver. It's all on you. And that's exactly why accountability is at the heart of the Empowerment Coaching Program.

In this program, we help phlebotomists transition from being skilled technicians to reliable business owners by embedding accountability into every part of the process. One way we do this is by setting clear expectations from the start. You and your coach co-create realistic goals, deadlines, and the action steps needed to reach them. If you consistently miss the mark—like skipping sessions, ignoring follow-up tasks, or showing up unprepared—there may be natural consequences such as rescheduling or pausing the coaching relationship. This isn't about discipline; it's about helping you recognize that how you show up for your coaching is a reflection of how you'll show up for your clients and your business.

Supportive Accountability: A Pathway to Progress

Accountability in the Empowerment Program is never about shame or blame. We understand that life happens—whether it's family emergencies, burnout, or feeling overwhelmed by all the hats you wear as a mobile phlebotomist. That's why our coaching model focuses on supportive accountability. Instead of judgment, we offer clarity, structure, and encouragement.

Let's say you were supposed to prepare your business intake forms this week, but it didn't happen. Your coach won't scold you—instead, they'll explore with you:

- What got in the way?

- Was the task unclear?

- Did you lack the tools or confidence?

Maybe you need a template to get started, or perhaps you're procrastinating because you're unsure how to brand your documents professionally. Rather than let the goal stall, your coach helps break it down:

- Draft a rough outline first.

- Schedule 20 minutes a day to work on it.

- Choose a deadline for review.

- Progress becomes doable, and momentum returns.

This kind of support is what builds long-term habits. You begin to feel more capable, not just in technical skills, but in time management, communication, and self-leadership—all essential to running a reputable and reliable mobile phlebotomy service.

"For God has not given us a spirit of fear, but of power and of love and of a sound mind."

— 2 Timothy 1:7

This verse reminds us that accountability isn't something to fear. It's a tool of empowerment. You are not meant to feel overwhelmed or paralyzed by expectations—you are equipped with power, love, and the discipline to rise. Coaching simply activates what God has already placed inside you.

Real-World Accountability: The Clients Are Watching

In phlebotomy, accountability shows up in real, tangible ways—especially when you're dealing with clients and providers. Missing an appointment doesn't just hurt your reputation; it can affect patient care. Delivering samples late or incorrectly handling them can compromise test results. These mistakes have consequences, not just for your business, but for real people's health.

That's why building strong habits—like confirming appointments the night before, double-checking supplies, and managing your schedule wisely—isn't just good practice; it's essential. The standards are high, and accountability helps you rise to meet them.

Adjusting Goals: When the Plan Isn't Working

In phlebotomy entrepreneurship, not every plan will go as expected—and that's okay. Sometimes your goal might be to land five new home health agency contracts in 60 days, only to find out that you're still stuck at zero by week eight. Rather than labeling that a failure, we treat it as feedback. The Empowerment Coaching Program includes scheduled milestone reviews—every 60 to 90 days—where you evaluate your progress with your coach and make data-informed adjustments.

This is where flexibility meets accountability. Maybe your marketing efforts need to shift from social media to in-person networking. Maybe your pricing package is confusing for prospective partners. Or maybe you underestimated how long credentialing with new healthcare providers takes. These are not signs that you're incapable—they're signs that your strategy needs refining.

Coaching helps you zoom out and make smart adjustments. You might reframe your original goal from "get five contracts" to "conduct ten outreach meetings and deliver three sample presentations." The actions are still ambitious, but now they're targeted and within reach. That's how your goals evolve with your business—not just bigger, but smarter.

Making Accountability a Daily Habit

Accountability isn't just something that happens during coaching calls—it's a mindset you carry into every part of your day. It's showing up on time, honoring your word, and learning from mistakes instead of hiding from them. It's checking in with yourself regularly:

- Did I follow through today?

- What did I avoid, and why?

- What small win can I celebrate, and what can I do better tomorrow?

You don't need to be perfect—you just need to be honest. The most successful phlebotomists aren't the ones who never mess up; they're the ones who own their progress, one step at a time.

Conclusion: Growth Through Ownership

Holding yourself accountable is not about pressure—it's about power. The power to change your life, one decision at a time. When you set clear goals, take consistent action, and hold yourself to your own standards, you're not just building a business—you're building trust in yourself.

In the Empowerment Coaching Program, we walk alongside you with grace, structure, and truth. Whether you're just starting out or refining your existing practice, accountability keeps you grounded, focused, and growing. The road ahead may have twists and setbacks—but with accountability, you're always moving forward.

References

1. Pettit, M. (2018). *The Importance of Accountability For Entrepreneurs*. Lucemi Consulting. Retrieved from https://lucemiconsulting.co.uk/accountability-for-entrepreneurs

2. Improve Medical. (2023). *Strategies for Quality Control in Phlebotomy Practices: Training, Audits, and Technology*. Retrieved from https://www.improve-medical.net/resources-2/Strategies-for-Quality-Control-in-Phlebotomy-Practices%3A-Training%2C-Audits%2C-and-Technology

3. ClinicalBasics. (2023). *Quality Assurance in Phlebotomy: Training, Audits, and Feedback Mechanisms for Patient Safety*. Retrieved from https://clinicalbasics.com/quality-assurance-in-phlebotomy-training-audits-and-feedback-mechanisms-for-patient-safety/

4. Saunsbury, E., & Howarth, G. (2016). *Improving communication between phlebotomists and doctors: a quality improvement project*. BMJ Quality Improvement Reports, 5(1), u206305.w4089. Retrieved from https://pmc.ncbi.nlm.nih.gov/articles/PMC5015820/

5. Batool, H., Mumtaz, A., Qadeer, S., & Bakht, Z. A. (2023). *Impact of Supervised Phlebotomy Training Programme on Performance Skills of Phlebotomy Staff*. AKEMU Journal. Retrieved from https://www.researchgate.net/publication/371166254_Impact_of_Supervised_Phlebotomy_Training_Programme_on_Performance_Skills_of_Phlebotomy_Staff

6. Sabady, C. (2019). *The Success of Creating a Phlebotomy Training Program Within an Organization.* ASCLS.

CHAPTER THREE
THE EMPOWERMENT BLUEPRINT FOR PHLEBOTOMISTS

Building a successful mobile phlebotomy business is more than just mastering the art of blood collection—it's about constructing a solid foundation that supports your entrepreneurial journey. In the Empowerment Coaching Program, we guide phlebotomists through the essential steps of establishing a business that is not only operational but also sustainable and poised for growth. This chapter delves into the critical components of creating a robust business plan, selecting the appropriate business structure, understanding the competitive landscape, and developing a strategic marketing plan.

Laying the Groundwork: Crafting Your Business Plan

A comprehensive business plan serves as the blueprint for your mobile phlebotomy service. It outlines your mission, defines your goals, and provides a roadmap for achieving them. The Empowerment Coaching Program emphasizes the importance of a well-thought-out plan to navigate the complexities of entrepreneurship.

"Commit your work to the Lord, and your plans will be established."

— Proverbs 16:3

This scripture reminds us that planning isn't just a practical exercise—it's a spiritual discipline. When you commit your efforts and your vision to God, you invite divine guidance into your business. It's not about building just any business; it's about building one with integrity, service, and purpose at its core.

Key Elements of a Mobile Phlebotomy Business Plan:

- **Executive Summary:** Summarize your business concept, mission, and vision.

- **Company Overview:** Detail your business structure, ownership, and the services you offer.

- **Market Analysis:** Research the demand for mobile phlebotomy services in your area.

- **Competitive Analysis:** Identify direct and indirect competitors and analyze their strengths and weaknesses.

- **Service Offerings:** Clearly define the services you provide, such as blood collection, wellness screenings, and therapeutic monitoring.

- **Marketing Strategy:** Outline how you plan to attract and retain clients.

- **Operational Plan:** Describe the day-to-day operations of your business, including logistics and staffing.

- **Financial Plan:** Provide projections for income, expenses, and profitability.

By developing each section thoughtfully, you create a roadmap that not only guides your actions but also instills confidence in potential investors and partners.

Choosing the Right Business Structure

Selecting the appropriate legal structure for your mobile phlebotomy business is a pivotal decision that impacts your liability, taxes, and operational flexibility. The Empowerment Coaching Program provides guidance on evaluating and choosing the structure that aligns with your goals and resources.

Common Business Structures:

- **Sole Proprietorship:** Simple to establish and offers complete control but comes with personal liability.

- **Limited Liability Company (LLC):** Provides liability protection and tax flexibility, making it a popular choice for small businesses.

- **Corporation:** Suitable for businesses seeking to raise capital through stock issuance but involves more regulatory requirements.

Each structure has its advantages and considerations. The Empowerment Coaching Program helps you assess your specific situation to make an informed choice.

Understanding the Competitive Landscape

In the mobile phlebotomy industry, understanding your competition is crucial for positioning your business effectively. The Empowerment Coaching Program emphasizes the importance of conducting a thorough competitive analysis to identify opportunities and threats.

Steps to Analyze Your Competition:

1. **Identify Competitors:** List both direct competitors (other mobile phlebotomy services) and indirect competitors (clinics, laboratories).

2. **Evaluate Strengths and Weaknesses:** Assess their service offerings, pricing, customer service, and market presence.

3. **Conduct a SWOT Analysis:** Identify your business's Strengths, Weaknesses, Opportunities, and Threats to understand your competitive edge.

By understanding the competitive landscape, you can differentiate your services and identify areas for improvement and innovation.

Developing a Strategic Marketing Plan

A well-crafted marketing plan is essential for attracting and retaining clients. The Empowerment Coaching Program guides phlebotomists in developing strategies that effectively communicate their value proposition to the target audience.

Components of a Marketing Plan:

- **Target Audience:** Define your ideal clients, such as homebound patients, elderly individuals, or healthcare facilities.

- **Branding:** Develop a strong brand identity that reflects professionalism and trustworthiness.

- **Digital Marketing:** Utilize SEO, social media, and online advertising to reach potential clients.

- **Networking:** Build relationships with healthcare providers and community organizations to generate referrals.

- **Promotions:** Offer introductory discounts or packages to attract new clients.

An effective marketing plan not only attracts clients but also builds long-term relationships that are vital for sustained success.

Implementing Operational Strategies

Efficient operations are the backbone of a successful mobile phlebotomy business. The Empowerment Coaching Program emphasizes the importance of streamlining processes to ensure smooth service delivery.

Key Operational Considerations:

- **Scheduling:** Implement a reliable system for booking appointments and managing time effectively.

- **Inventory Management:** Maintain adequate supplies and equipment to meet client needs without overstocking.

- **Quality Control:** Establish protocols to ensure high standards of service and compliance with health regulations.

- **Customer Service:** Train staff to provide compassionate and professional service to clients.

By focusing on operational excellence, you enhance client satisfaction and operational efficiency.

Financial Planning and Sustainability

Financial stability is crucial for the longevity of your mobile phlebotomy business. The Empowerment Coaching Program assists phlebotomists in developing financial plans that support growth and sustainability.

Financial Planning Steps:

1. **Budgeting:** Estimate startup costs, including equipment, licensing, and marketing expenses.

2. **Revenue Projections:** Forecast income based on service pricing and expected client volume.

3. **Expense Management:** Monitor ongoing expenses to maintain profitability.

4. **Funding Options:** Explore funding sources, such as loans or grants, to support business expansion.

A solid financial plan ensures that you r business remains viable and can adapt to changing market conditions.

Steps to Becoming an Entrepreneur in Your Field

To fully step into your role as a business owner, especially in healthcare-adjacent fields like phlebotomy, laboratory work, or medication services, there are essential steps and credentials to secure. Whether or not you plan to operate a lab or process bloodwork specimens, understanding the structure is vital.

Note: Some businesses may require CLIA certification (Clinical Laboratory Improvement Amendments). While not mandatory for all, it is essential for handling and processing bloodwork or lab specimens. You don't have to have CLIA unless your work involves diagnostics, but it's an option to explore if you expand your services.

Foundational Requirements

1. **Plan** – Define your business model, niche, and service offerings.

2. **Business Name** – Choose a unique, professional name.

3. **Business Structure** – Register as an **LLC** (Limited Liability Company) or **Corporation** based on your needs.

4. **EIN Number** – Apply for an Employer Identification Number with the **IRS**.

5. **Insurance** – Secure business liability and professional insurance.

6. **Business Bank Account** – Open an account in your business name.

7. **Payment System** – Set up a **Visa/MasterCard** merchant account or POS system to receive payments.

8. **NPI Number** – Apply for a **National Provider Identifier** if your business is healthcare-related.

9. **Hospital or Clinic Approval** – If required, seek partnerships or verification with approved medical facilities.

10. **Licenses** – Obtain any necessary business or health-related **state licenses**.

Conclusion

Establishing a mobile phlebotomy business requires careful planning, strategic decision-making, and a commitment to excellence. The Empowerment Coaching Program provides phlebotomists with the tools and guidance needed to build a strong foundation for their entrepreneurial endeavors. By focusing on comprehensive business planning, understanding the competitive landscape, developing effective marketing strategies, and implementing efficient operations, you position your business for success in the growing mobile healthcare industry.

References

1. **U.S. Small Business Administration (SBA).** (n.d.). *Write your business plan.*
   Retrieved from: https://www.sba.gov/business-guide/plan-your-business/write-your-business-plan

2. **Internal Revenue Service (IRS).** (n.d.). *Apply for an Employer Identification Number (EIN) online.*
   Retrieved from: https://www.irs.gov/businesses/small-businesses-self-employed/apply-for-an-employer-identification-number-ein-online

3. **Centers for Medicare & Medicaid Services (CMS).** (n.d.). *National Provider Identifier (NPI) Registry.*
   Retrieved from: https://nppes.cms.hhs.gov/

4. Kotler, P., & Keller, K. L. (2016). *Marketing Management* (15th ed.). Pearson Education.

   A foundational text on marketing strategy, branding, and digital outreach relevant for small healthcare businesses.

5. McKeever, M. (2022). *How to Write a Business Plan* (14th ed.). Nolo Press.

Offers detailed guidance on crafting business plans for startups and small businesses, including service-based operations like mobile phlebotomy.

6. Osterwalder, A., & Pigneur, Y. (2010). *Business Model Generation: A Handbook for Visionaries, Game Changers, and Challengers*. Wiley.

   Helps entrepreneurs understand and build sustainable business models, including service innovation.

7. Harvard Business Review. (n.d.). *A Refresher on SWOT Analysis*.
   Retrieved from: https://hbr.org/2016/01/a-refresher-on-swot-analysis

8. American Association for Clinical Chemistry (AACC). (n.d.). *Requirements for Starting a Laboratory or Phlebotomy Service*.
   Retrieved from: https://www.aacc.org/science-and-research

9. Google for Small Business. (n.d.). *Build your presence online*.
   Retrieved from: https://smallbusiness.withgoogle.com/

10. Bplans. (n.d.). *Phlebotomy Business Plan Example*.
    Retrieved from: https://www.bplans.com/phlebotomy-business-plan/

CHAPTER FOUR
EMPOWERMENT &
DETERMINATION

Empowerment is not merely a concept; it's the driving force that propels you from being a skilled phlebotomist to a successful mobile healthcare entrepreneur. It requires more than technical proficiency; it demands a mindset that embraces growth, resilience, and strategic action. In this chapter, we delve into the mindset shifts and actionable strategies that will empower you to build a thriving mobile phlebotomy business.

Claiming Your Authority: The Entrepreneurial Mindset

Transitioning from a phlebotomist to a business owner is a profound shift in identity. It's about stepping into your role as a leader, not just in healthcare but in your own professional journey. This transformation involves:

- **Embracing Ownership:** Recognize that every decision, from scheduling to client relations, is within your control. Your choices define your business's success.

- **Cultivating Confidence:** Trust in your abilities and knowledge. Confidence is contagious and builds trust with clients and partners alike.

- **Fostering Resilience:** The path of entrepreneurship is fraught with challenges. Resilience allows you to navigate setbacks and continue moving forward.

By adopting this mindset, you position yourself not just as a service provider but as a trusted healthcare professional leading a business.

Goal Setting: From Vision to Action

Empowerment thrives on clear, actionable goals. These goals serve as the roadmap for your business journey, guiding you through both short-term tasks and long-term aspirations.

- **Long-Term Vision:** Define where you see your business in the next 3 to 5 years. This could include expanding service areas, diversifying services, or building a team.

- **Short-Term Objectives:** Break down your long-term vision into achievable milestones. For instance, securing your first five clients, establishing partnerships with local clinics, or implementing a digital booking system.

- **SMART Goals:** Ensure your goals are Specific, Measurable, Achievable, Relevant, and Time-bound. This framework provides clarity and direction.

Regularly revisiting and adjusting these goals ensures they remain aligned with your evolving business landscape.

Building a Resilient Entrepreneurial Mindset

Resilience is the cornerstone of entrepreneurial success. It's the ability to adapt, learn, and persevere in the face of challenges. And when fear, self-doubt, or overwhelm try to creep in, you can anchor yourself in this truth:

"Fear not, for I am with you;
be not dismayed, for I am your God.
I will strengthen you, I will help you,
I will uphold you with my righteous right hand."

— **Isaiah 41:10**

This promise offers more than comfort—it offers courage. Building a business is demanding, but you are never doing it alone. God's presence brings the strength to stand back up, even after setbacks. With faith as your foundation, resilience becomes more than grit; it becomes grace in action.

Strategies for Building Resilience:

- **Continuous Learning:** Stay updated with the latest in phlebotomy practices, healthcare regulations, and business management. This knowledge enhances your service quality and operational efficiency.

- **Networking:** Connect with other healthcare professionals, attend industry events, and engage in online communities. Networking opens doors to opportunities and collaborations.

- **Self-Care:** Managing a business can be demanding. Prioritize your well-being to maintain the energy and focus needed to lead effectively.

A resilient mindset not only helps you overcome obstacles but also positions you as a reliable and adaptable service provider.

Embracing Adaptability: Navigating Business Growth

As your mobile phlebotomy business expands, adaptability becomes crucial. The healthcare landscape is dynamic, and staying flexible allows you to seize new opportunities and address emerging challenges.

- **Technology Integration:** Leverage digital tools for scheduling, client management, and billing. This streamlines operations and enhances client experience.

- **Service Diversification:** Consider offering additional services like wellness screenings or home healthcare support to meet the diverse needs of your clients.

- **Scalability:** Plan for growth by developing systems that can handle increased demand, such as standardized procedures and training programs for new staff.

Adaptability ensures your business remains competitive and responsive to the changing needs of the healthcare industry.

Cultivating a Mindset of Continuous Improvement

Empowerment is a journey of continuous growth. Cultivating a mindset of improvement involves:

- **Seeking Feedback:** Regularly solicit input from clients and partners to identify areas for enhancement.

- **Reflecting on Experiences:** Take time to assess what strategies are working and where adjustments are needed.

- **Investing in Development:** Pursue further education and training to expand your skill set and knowledge base.

A commitment to continuous improvement fosters innovation and positions your business as a leader in mobile phlebotomy services.

Conclusion: Empowerment as the Path to Success

Empowerment is the catalyst that transforms challenges into opportunities. By adopting an entrepreneurial mindset, setting clear goals, building resilience, embracing adaptability, and committing to continuous improvement, you lay the foundation for a successful mobile phlebotomy business.

Let Isaiah 41:10 serve as your reminder: you are not alone. With every challenge, God offers strength. With every new step, He provides guidance. Empowerment is not a destination but a continuous journey of growth, faith, and achievement.

References

1. Wikipedia contributors. (2025). *Entrepreneurship*. Wikipedia. Retrieved from https://en.wikipedia.org/wiki/Entrepreneurship

2. Wikipedia contributors. (2025). *Resilience (psychological)*. Wikipedia. Retrieved from https://en.wikipedia.org/wiki/Resilience_(psychological)

3. MindTools. (2025). *SMART Goals: How to Make Your Goals Achievable*. Retrieved from https://www.mindtools.com/pages/article/newHTE_90.htm

4. The Knowledge Academy. (2025). *Developing a Growth Mindset in Business*. Retrieved from https://www.theknowledgeacademy.com/blog/developing-growth-mindset-business/

5. Harvard Business Review. (2025). *How to Develop a Leadership Mindset.* Retrieved from https://hbr.org/2020/09/how-to-develop-a-leadership-mindset

6. Gallup. (2025). *Why Resilient Entrepreneurs Succeed More Often.* Retrieved from https://www.gallup.com/workplace/

7. Learn Business. (2025). *How to Set Business Goals that Drive Growth and Confidence.* Retrieved from https://learn-business.org/goal-setting/business-growth

8. Robin Waite. (2025). *Empowering Entrepreneurs Through Mindset Shifts.* Retrieved from https://www.robinwaite.com/blog/empowering-entrepreneurs-through-mindset

9. Forbes. (2025). *Adaptability in Business: A Key to Long-Term Success.* Retrieved from https://www.forbes.com/sites/forbesbusinesscouncil/

10. EMOCARE. (2025). *Building Entrepreneurial Resilience in Health Professionals.* Retrieved from https://emocare.co.in/entrepreneurial-resilience

CHAPTER FIVE
TRUSTING GOD'S GUIDANCE

Building a thriving mobile phlebotomy business demands more than technical skills and business savvy—it requires deep inner strength and unwavering faith. Faith is not a peripheral idea; it's the cornerstone that grounds every coaching conversation, decision, and milestone. This chapter explores how integrating faith into coaching empowers mobile phlebotomists to navigate uncertainty, build resilience, and maintain focus on their calling.

Faith as a Guiding Light in the Coaching Journey

Entrepreneurship, especially in healthcare services like mobile phlebotomy, often involves unpredictable challenges—whether it's securing consistent clients, managing complex regulations, or balancing the demands of a growing business. These hurdles can feel overwhelming. That's why faith is emphasized as a vital source of guidance and empowerment throughout the coaching process.

Unlike generic business coaching, this approach frames faith as a source of empowerment and peace. It helps phlebotomists internalize the truth found in **Deuteronomy 8:18**:

"But remember the Lord your God, for it is He who gives you the ability to produce wealth, and so confirms His covenant, which He swore to your ancestors, as it is today."

This verse becomes more than just encouragement—it's a powerful reminder that the ability to build a business, to create impact and generate income, is a divine gift. Even when the journey feels uncertain or slow, it's grounded in a covenant that affirms your God-given ability to succeed.

Coaching Mobile Phlebotomists with Faith in Mind

In this faith-centered coaching model, phlebotomists are invited to lean into a dual process: spiritual grounding paired with actionable business coaching. This unique combination equips them to:

- **Cultivate patience and perseverance** during slow growth phases, recognizing that divine timing often differs from human expectations.

- **Stay motivated through setbacks** by anchoring their efforts in a higher purpose beyond just profit or metrics.

- **Build confidence and clarity** when facing decisions, knowing their coaching journey respects and incorporates their faith values.

- **Transform anxiety into hopeful action**, by setting faith-inspired goals that align with their mission to serve clients compassionately and professionally.

For example, if a phlebotomist struggles to grow their client base, the coach will explore not only practical barriers—such as marketing tactics or networking strategies—but also the spiritual question: "How is your faith shaping your vision for this business? Where do you see God working in this challenge?" This holistic approach allows clients to find renewed clarity and motivation rooted in belief.

Faith and Action: A Balanced Partnership

It is important to understand that faith is not passive. Trusting God does not mean waiting idly; it means taking consistent, purposeful steps while remaining spiritually anchored.

Through coaching, phlebotomists learn to:

- Break down their long-term vision into small, faith-driven goals.

- Celebrate incremental progress as evidence of God's provision.

- Cultivate resilience by viewing obstacles as opportunities for spiritual and professional growth.

- Practice daily affirmations that reinforce trust and courage.

This balance between faith and practical action distinguishes successful mobile phlebotomists from those who become discouraged or stagnant.

Unique Advantages of a Faith-Integrated Coaching Model

This faith-based coaching approach offers several key advantages tailored to mobile phlebotomists:

- **Holistic Growth:** Supporting not only technical skill development and business growth, but also personal spiritual development.

- **Emotional Resilience:** By rooting challenges in faith, phlebotomists build mental toughness to face daily uncertainties.

- **Purpose-Driven Motivation:** Knowing their work serves a higher purpose increases job satisfaction and client empathy.

- **Community and Support:** Many coaching programs connect participants with fellow faith-driven entrepreneurs, fostering encouragement and accountability.

Ultimately, this approach helps phlebotomists embrace the full identity of "successful entrepreneur and compassionate healthcare professional."

Conclusion: Empowerment Through Faith and Coaching

Faith is not an afterthought—it is the foundation that empowers mobile phlebotomists to rise, adapt, and thrive. Trusting God's timing and guidance creates the calm confidence needed to navigate the challenges of entrepreneurship. Combined with practical coaching on business skills, accountability, and goal-setting, this faith-infused approach prepares phlebotomists to build sustainable, purpose-driven mobile phlebotomy businesses.

As you journey through your own mobile phlebotomy career, remember: faith is your anchor, coaching is your compass, and empowerment is your destination.

References

1. Bible Gateway. (2025). Proverbs 3:5-6. Bible Gateway. Retrieved from https://www.biblegateway.com/passage/?search=Proverbs+3%3A5-6&version=NIV

2. Bible Gateway. (2025). James 2:26. Bible Gateway. Retrieved from https://www.biblegateway.com/passage/?search=James+2%3A26&version=NIV

3. The Knowledge Academy. (2025). What is Coaching? A Comprehensive Guide. Retrieved from https://www.theknowledgeacademy.com/blog/what-is-coaching/

4. HR Fraternity. (2025). Empowering Clients to Set Achievable Goals in Coaching Sessions. Retrieved from https://www.hrfraternity.com/health-excellence/empowering-clients-to-set-achievable-goals-in-coaching-sessions.html

5. Robin Waite. (2025). Cultivating Progress: Strategies for Effectively Coaching Clients. Retrieved from https://www.robinwaite.com/blog/cultivating-progress-strategies-for-effectively-coaching-clients

6. EMOCARE. (2025). Accountability Coaching: Achieving Goals with Support and Guidance. Retrieved from https://emocare.co.in/accountability-coaching

Epilogue

As you close this book, it's important to pause and reflect on the deeper journey you've undertaken—not just the practical steps, but the personal transformation at the core of building a mobile phlebotomy business.

Empowerment is more than a buzzword; it's a commitment to owning your role as a healthcare entrepreneur with confidence and integrity. It means recognizing that success is not solely measured by numbers or contracts, but by the consistency with which you show up, the quality of care you provide, and the resilience you cultivate in the face of challenges.

This journey reminds us that entrepreneurship in healthcare is uniquely demanding. You balance clinical expertise with business operations, navigate regulations, build relationships, and manage the delicate balance between work and well-being. None of this happens overnight, and none of it is easy—but it is deeply rewarding.

Coaching and accountability serve as your compass and engine. They help you stay aligned with your vision while pushing you gently to stretch beyond your comfort zones. This support system transforms potential overwhelm into manageable steps and turns setbacks into lessons.

Moreover, cultivating a mindset of faith grounds your journey in something larger than yourself. It's faith that sustains when uncertainty clouds your path, that encourages patience when results are slow to come, and that fuels hope when challenges mount. Faith, paired with action, creates a powerful dynamic where perseverance meets divine timing.

"Now he who supplies seed to the sower and bread for food will also supply and increase your store of seed and will enlarge the harvest of your righteousness."

— 2 Corinthians 9:10

This verse is a powerful reminder that your efforts are not in vain. As you plant the seeds of service, excellence, and commitment in your business, trust that God will provide the growth. Your work has impact beyond what you see—touching lives, building trust, and creating ripples of wellness in your community.

Remember that building a successful mobile phlebotomy business is not just a career choice—it's a calling. You are positioned to serve your community in profound ways, providing care that is accessible and compassionate. Your commitment to excellence and empowerment enriches the healthcare ecosystem and enhances the lives of your clients.

As you move forward, keep nurturing the habits of preparation, accountability, adaptability, and faith. Continue to seek mentorship, embrace learning, and celebrate every small victory. These daily practices will build a foundation strong enough to support your growth for years to come.

Thank you for committing to this path. May the principles and insights shared in this program serve you well. May you thrive as a skilled phlebotomist, a savvy entrepreneur, and a person of purpose.

Your journey of empowerment has only just begun.

Q1. What is your goal?

Q2. What are your plans going forward?

Q3. How can this book apply to your lifestyle?

Q4. Do u have a name for your business?

Q5. Would u like to start your own business?

Case Studies

Camilla Henderson –
From Technician to Trusted Mobile Phlebotomist

Background:

Camilla Henderson, a certified phlebotomist from New Orleans, recognized a gap in healthcare accessibility and decided to make a difference. She founded Allimac Mobile LLC, aiming to provide convenient blood draw services to individuals unable to visit traditional clinics.

Challenges Faced:

- **Diverse Clientele:** Serving a wide range of patients, from homebound individuals to busy professionals, required adaptability and personalized care.

- **Safety Concerns:** Operating in areas with high crime rates necessitated strict safety protocols, including carrying a license to ensure personal security during home visits.

- **Emotional Boundaries:** Developing emotional connections with patients, like her first patient Mr. Phil, highlighted the importance of maintaining professional boundaries to prevent burnout.

Key Success Factors:

- **Tailored Services:** Understanding the unique needs of each neighborhood allowed Camilla to offer customized services, such as accepting cash in lower-income areas and card payments in affluent neighborhoods.

- **Thorough Verification:** Implementing strict verification processes, including requiring physical doctor's orders and confirming them directly with physicians, ensured the legitimacy and safety of each appointment.

- **Emotional Intelligence:** Learning to manage emotional attachments helped maintain professional integrity and personal well-being.

Personal Insight:

Camilla emphasizes the importance of preparation and adaptability in mobile phlebotomy. She advises fellow phlebotomists to understand their clients' environments and needs, ensuring both safety and satisfaction.

MYRNA STEINBAUM –
INNOVATING MOBILE PHLEBOTOMY SERVICES

Background:

Myrna Steinbaum, the founder of VeniExpress in Southern California, transformed the traditional phlebotomy model by offering mobile services that cater to both individual patients and corporate clients.

Challenges Faced:

- **Service Diversification:** Expanding services to include drug testing and diagnostic imaging required significant investment in equipment and training.

- **Market Penetration:** Establishing a brand in a competitive market demanded innovative marketing strategies and exceptional customer service.

- **Operational Logistics:** Coordinating appointments and managing a mobile workforce posed logistical challenges that required efficient systems and processes.

Key Success Factors:

- **Comprehensive Service Offerings:** By providing a range of services beyond blood draws, VeniExpress attracted a broader clientele, including businesses requiring on-site drug testing.

- **Strategic Partnerships:** Collaborating with healthcare providers and employers expanded the company's reach and credibility.

- **Customer-Centric Approach:** Prioritizing patient comfort and convenience led to high satisfaction rates and repeat business.

Personal Insight:

Myrna advises aspiring mobile phlebotomists to focus on building strong relationships with clients and continuously seek opportunities for service diversification. She believes that understanding and meeting the evolving needs of the community is key to sustained success.

Conclusion:

These case studies illustrate that success in mobile phlebotomy requires more than technical skills; it demands adaptability, emotional intelligence, strategic planning, and a deep commitment to patient care. Aspiring phlebotomists can draw valuable lessons from Camilla and Myrna's experiences to navigate their entrepreneurial journeys effectively.

ROLE-PLAY -
SCENARIO ACTIVITIES

Purpose:

To help aspiring mobile phlebotomists develop the communication, emotional intelligence, and professionalism needed to thrive in real-world situations. These activities simulate common encounters that require quick thinking, empathy, and business-savvy confidence.

Scenario 1:
Calming a Nervous Client

Situation:

You arrive at a client's home for a scheduled blood draw. The client opens the door looking anxious and hesitant. They express fear of needles and mention a previous bad experience with a phlebotomist.

Prompt for Response:

- What do you say to put them at ease?
- How do you establish trust quickly?

- What tone, body language, or reassurances would you use?

Coaching Tip:

Start with empathy. Use calm, confident language and validate their concerns. Offer to explain the process step-by-step and ensure you listen without rushing. Personalize your approach based on the client's comfort level.

Suggested Practice Response:

"I completely understand—it's okay to feel nervous. I've worked with a lot of clients who've had similar experiences, and my goal is to make this as comfortable as possible for you. We can take it one step at a time, and I'll explain everything before I do it."

Scenario 2:
Pitching to a Physician's Office

Situation:

You walk into a local physician's office to introduce your mobile phlebotomy services. The front desk staff and the office manager seem uncertain about partnering with an independent phlebotomist.

Prompt for Response:

- What's your opening pitch?
- How do you address their concerns about reliability and professionalism?
- What makes your service valuable to them?

Coaching Tip:

Focus on the pain points you solve—flexibility, convenience, reduced burden on in-office staff, faster patient turnaround. Confidence, clear communication, and well-prepared marketing materials go a long way.

Suggested Practice Response:

"I provide mobile phlebotomy services that support your practice by helping patients who can't easily come in for labs—homebound individuals, seniors, or post-surgical patients. I follow HIPAA-compliant protocols, and I'm CLIA-waiver certified. This could help your team focus more on in-office care while still ensuring your patients get timely lab work done."

Scenario 3:
Handling a Scheduling Conflict

Situation:

You realize you double-booked two clients on the same morning—both expecting you within 30 minutes of each other.

Prompt for Response:

- How do you handle the error professionally?
- What do you communicate to the clients?
- How do you prevent this from happening again?

Coaching Tip:

Accountability and transparency build trust. Don't make excuses—own the mistake and provide a clear plan to fix it. Then put systems in place to avoid future overlaps.

Suggested Practice Response:

"Hi [Client Name], I want to sincerely apologize—I made a scheduling error and I want to make this right. I can be at your location by [X time] or I can reschedule at your convenience. I appreciate your patience, and I've already updated my system to ensure this doesn't happen again."

Scenario 4:
Managing an Upset Patient

Situation:

A patient complains that their results are delayed and blames you, even though the lab was responsible.

Prompt for Response:

- How do you respond without deflecting blame?

- How do you protect your professional image?

- What steps do you take to resolve the situation?

Coaching Tip:

Stay calm, professional, and solution-oriented. While it may not be your fault, the client sees you as their point of contact. Offer to follow up and keep them updated.

Suggested Practice Response:

"Thank you for bringing this to my attention—I completely understand your concern. While I don't control the lab's timeline, I'll personally reach out to them right away and keep you posted. My goal is to make sure you're not left in the dark."

Scenario 5:
Promoting Your Services at a Community Event

Situation:

You've set up a booth at a local health fair. Visitors keep walking by without stopping. You need to draw attention and connect with potential clients or partners.

Prompt for Response:

- What's your 30-second elevator pitch?
- How do you make your service memorable?
- What visual or verbal hook do you use?

Coaching Tip:

Energy and clarity matter. Your messaging should be direct and solution-focused. Consider having printed flyers, testimonials, or even a visual demonstration (e.g., sample kits).

Suggested Practice Response:

"Hi! I run a mobile phlebotomy service that brings lab testing right to your door. No waiting rooms, no hassle. We serve individuals, seniors, and even employers needing onsite testing. Quick, convenient, and CLIA-compliant. Let me show you how easy it is!"

How to Use These Activities

1. **Reflection:** After role-playing each scenario, reflect using these questions:

    o   What did I do well?

    o   What could I have done differently?

    o   How can I prepare better for a similar situation?

2. **Group Practice:** If you're in a study group or coaching cohort, practice these scenarios together. Take turns being the client and the phlebotomist.

3. **Journaling:** Write down your responses and feelings. Journaling helps solidify your learning and recognize emotional patterns or growth areas.

About The Author

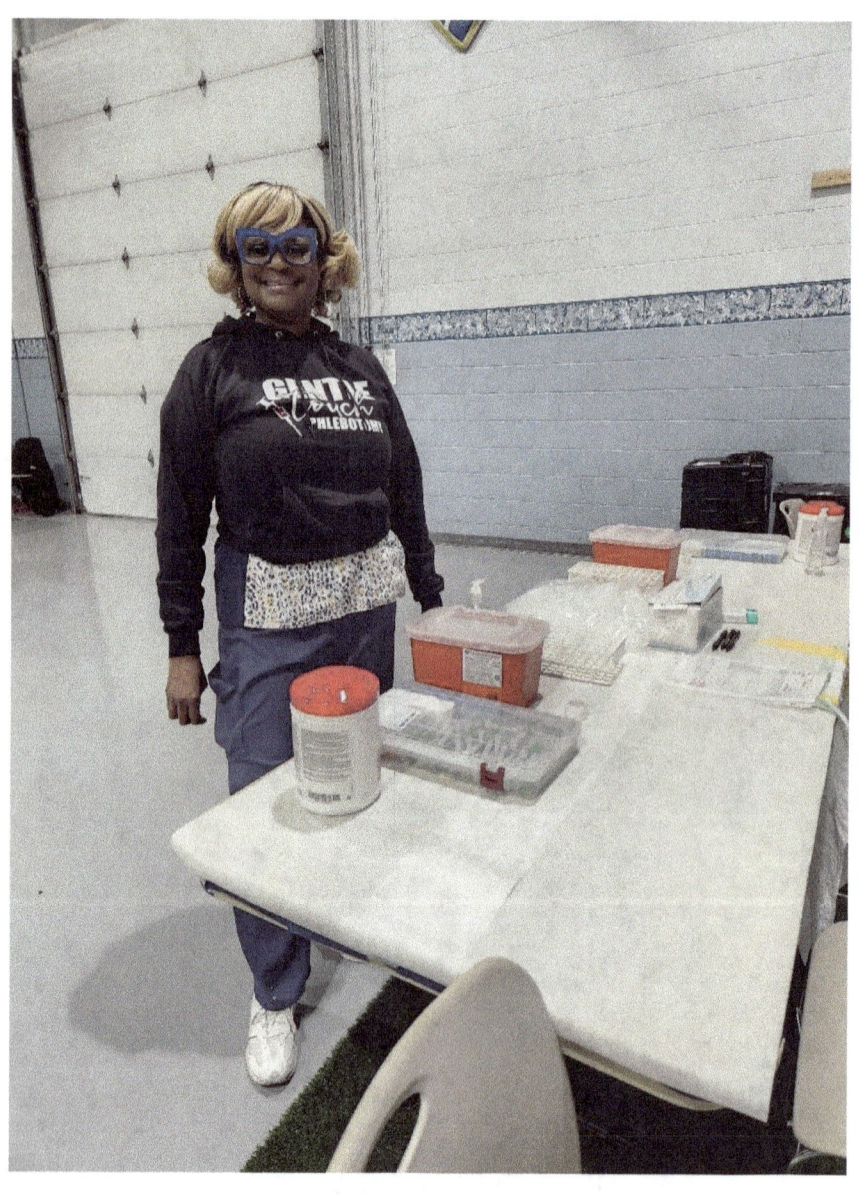

Things to require while availing our services:

1 Plan ---

2 Business name LLC or corporate ----------------------------

3 EIN number IRS ------------------------------------

4 Insurance --------------------------------------

5 Bank account business name --------------------------------

6 Visa credit so u can receive payment -------------------------

7 Your nip number ---------------------------------------

8. Hospital Approved clinic --

9. License from your State ----------------------------------